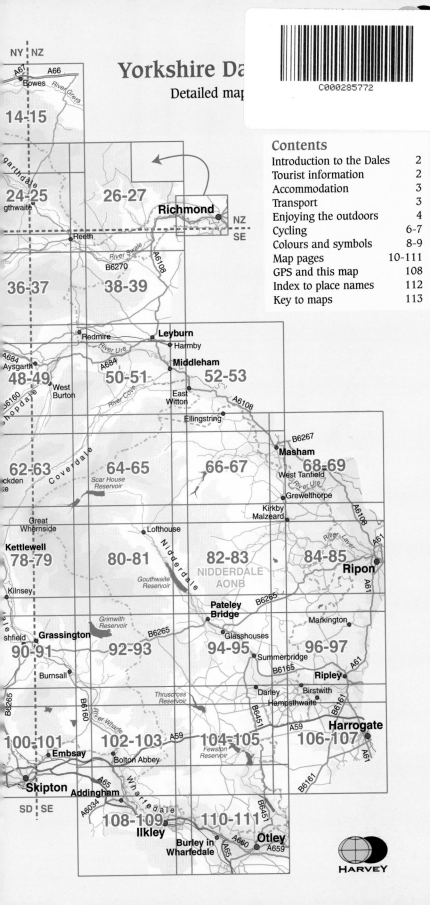

Yorkshire Da[les]

Detailed ma[p]

C000285772

Contents

HARVEY

How to Use the Outdoor Atlas

This Outdoor Atlas combines in one volume detailed maps of the Yorkshire Dales, including the whole of the National Park and the Nidderdale Area of Outstanding Natural Beauty. The map inside the front cover shows the area covered and how the individual pages run from one to another. There is an overlap of 1.4km between pages. See the contents (see p.1) for where to find other information, key to map symbols etc.

The Outdoor Atlas is designed for outdoor use. Although not tear-proof, the pages are printed on waterproof paper. If your Outdoor Atlas gets wet just hang it up to drip dry!

The maps are detailed, making them suitable for walkers and cyclists, and a useful reference for residents and visitors. The book is a handy size for carrying in a map case or map pocket or on a bike map holder. It is spiral bound to lie flat in the hand.

The Yorkshire Dales - A National Treasure for All to Enjoy

The Yorkshire Dales is a varied and beautiful area stretching from Kirkby Lonsdale in the west to Ripon in the east. It covers approximately 1,700 square miles, the core of which is the Yorkshire Dales National Park.

The Dales includes some of the finest upland scenery in the country, promising enjoyment whatever the season. They are famed for their rich mosaic of flower-filled meadows, high fells, heather moors and limestone scenery, scattered with stone barns, drystone walls and an abundance of waterfalls. Cradled in the valley bottoms, stone-built villages guard centuries of history. In these thriving rural communities agriculture and tourism play a vital role in maintaining the area's economy. Throughout the year the Dales' artists and craftspeople can be seen at work - while local food and drink producers stock many of the region's pubs, shops and cafes.

Please remember that the Yorkshire Dales landscape is sensitive, and is not indestructible. It requires constant conservation work to protect and enhance its natural beauty, wildlife and cultural heritage. The local authorities of the area work to provide the best possible facilities for residents and visitors alike. Please help them to conserve valuable resources by following the Country Code (see p.4).

To get the very best out of your visit to the Yorkshire Dales, contact one of the area's National Park or Tourist Information Centres. Services include accommodation booking, maps, information guides, souvenirs and a free newspaper 'The Visitor', which lists events and attractions in the area. The staff working in the National Park and Tourist Information Centres have a wealth of knowledge and interesting information about the area, including where to buy local produce or find that special gift.

National Park & Tourist Information Centres

Aysgarth	tel: 01969 663424	email: aysgarth@ytbtic.co.uk
Bedale	tel: 01677 424604	email: bedale@ytbtic.co.uk
Grassington	tel: 01756 752774	email: grassington@ytbtic.co.uk
Harrogate	tel: 01423 537300	email: tic@harrogate.gov.uk
Hawes	tel: 01969 667450	email: hawes@ytbtic.co.uk
Horton in Ribblesdale	tel: 01729 860333	email: horton@ytbtic.co.uk
Ilkley	tel: 01943 602319	email: ilkleytic@bradford.gov.uk
Ingleton	tel: 01524 241049	email; ingleton@ytbtic.co.uk
Kirkby Lonsdale	tel: 01524 271437	email: kltic@southlakeland.gov.uk
Kirkby Stephen	tel: 01768 371199	email: ks.tic@eden.gov.uk
Leyburn	tel: 01969 623069	email: leyburn@ytbtic.co.uk
Malham	tel: 01729 830363	email: malham@ytbtic.co.uk
Otley	tel: 0113 247 7707	email: otleytic@leedslearning.net
Pateley Bridge	tel: 01423 711147	email: pateleybridge@ytbtic.co.uk
Reeth	tel: 01748 884059	email: reeth@ytbtic.co.uk
Richmond	tel: 01748 850252	email: richmond@ytbtic.co.uk
Ripon	tel: 01765 604625	email: ripontic@harrogate.gov.uk
Sedbergh	tel: 01539 620125	email: sedbergh@yorkshiredales.org.uk
Settle	tel: 01729 825192	email: settle@ytbtic.co.uk
Skipton	tel: 01756 792809	email: skipton@ytbtic.co.uk

Accommodation

Various types of accommodation are available in the area from bed and breakfast to inns, guesthouses and hotels. There are also many youth hostels, bunkhouse barns and camp-sites, plus a variety of accommodation including .

A free Yorkshire Dales Accommodation Guide is available from National Park Centres and information points. Alternatively from:

Hawes National Park Centre, Station Yard, Hawes, N. Yorks DL8 3NT. Tel: 01969 667450
Fax: 01969 667165 Email: Hawes@ytbtic.co.uk www.yorkshiredales.org
With the exception of campsites, it is best to book in advance.

YOUTH HOSTELS

Dent	tel: 01539 625251
Grinton	tel: 01748 884206
Hawes	tel: 01969 667368
Ingleton	tel: 0870 770 5880
Keld	tel: 01748 886259
Kettlewell	tel: 01756 760232
Malham	tel: 01729 830321
Stainforth	tel: 01729 823577

For information on all hostels in England and Wales contact www.yha.org.uk .

INDEPENDENT HOSTELS

There are independently run hostels and bunkhouses in the area. An annual guide is published by: The Backpackers Press Tel: 01629 580427
www.independenthostelguide.co.uk

CAMPING

There are a number of campsites in the area. Do not camp without permission. For information contact a National Park or Tourist Information Centre (see above or p.2).

Money, Food and Water

All small towns and most villages have places to buy food or get a meal. Please note that grocery stores may not be open after 5.30pm. If walking or cycling, remember to carry enough to drink. It is not advisable to drink from streams.

Public Transport to and through the Dales

Free timetables and maps containing all bus and train services to and within the Yorkshire Dales are available from all National Park and Tourist Information Centres, by post: National Park and Tourist Information Centre, Station Yard, Hawes, North Yorkshire, DL8 3NT, or by email: hawes@ytbtic.co.uk or tel: 01969 667450.

For timetable enquiries please call the National Traveline tel: 0870 608 2 608 or see the jouney planner at www.traveline.org.uk. Additional information can be obtained from the Yorkshire Dales National Park Authority website
www.yorkshiredales.org.uk and www.dalesbus.org.
National Rail enquiries tel: 08457 48 49 50 or www.nationalrail.co.uk
National Express Coach Services tel: 08705 808080 or www.nationalexpress.com

Driving in the Yorkshire Dales

Roads in the Yorkshire Dales are generally narrow with frequent bends and often lined with dry-stone walls. Always be on the look out for animals, walkers and cyclists.

Parking

Always use managed car parks marked on the map. Unfortunately informally or remotely parked cars are targets for car crime. Do not park on verges, in gateways, passing places and outside houses as this can cause damage and obstructions.

Enjoying the Outdoors in the Yorkshire Dales

COUNTRY CODE

Guard against all risk of fire
Fasten all gates
Keep your dogs under close control
Keep to public paths across farmland
Enjoy the countryside and respect its life and work
Use gates and stiles to cross fences, hedges and walls
Leave livestock, crops and machinery alone
Take your litter home
Help to keep all water clean
Protect wildlife, plants and trees
Take special care on country roads
Make no unnecessary noise

ACCESS

Most land is privately owned. Observe the Country Code. Rights of Way (public foot-paths and bridleways) are generally waymarked throughout the Yorkshire Dales National Park and Nidderdale AONB by various signs. Where coloured arrows are used on the ground they signify the following:
- Yellow arrow: Public footpath; walkers only (no bikes or horses)
- Blue arrow: Public bridleway; walking, cycling and horse riding
- Red arrow: Byway; walking, cycling, riding and motor vehicles

LITTER

Litter is not only an eyesore but a risk to wild and farm animals. Please carry all litter to a litter bin or disposal point.

WEATHER

TGO Weathercall: www.weathercall.co.uk
North East England tel: 09068 111348
Cumbria and Lake District tel: 09068 111349
Met Office: www.meto.gov.uk

FIRES

Please do not light fires. Fire risk at certain times of year is extremely high. If, in an emergency, you must light one, please take great care. Never light a fire on top of vegetation and do not damage living wood for fuel. Please leave the site safe and remove all traces of the fire.

Global Positioning System

This map can be used with GPS. The pale grey grid on the map is the National Grid in 1km squares. The National Grid numbers are in the frame around the map. Set your GPS receiver to Map Datum OSGB and the position format to British Grid (see also p.108).

Index to Town Plans

Maps of the Yorkshire Dales

For up to date information contact a National Park or Tourist Information Centre, visit the HARVEY web shop: **www.harveymaps.co.uk** or call the HARVEY hotline: **01786 841202**

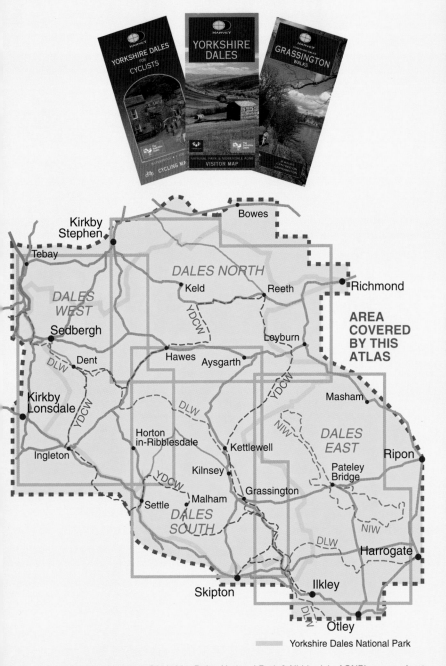

Yorkshire Dales National Park

★ Maps covering the whole area (Yorkshire Dales National Park & Nidderdale AONB) on one sheet:-
Yorkshire Dales Visitor Map, Yorkshire Dales for Cyclists

★ Maps for walking & cycling (including off road cycle routes):-
Dales South, Dales North, Dales East, Dales West

★ Walks - each map has 8 graded routes:-
Grassington, Hawes, Pateley Bridge, Reeth, Sedbergh, Settle

★ Long distance routes:-
Yorkshire Dales Cycle Way (YDCW), Nidderdale Way (NIW), Dales Way (DLW)

Cycling in the Yorkshire Dales

TOURING CYCLING

The Yorkshire Dales area provides some of the country's finest cycling. You can devise routes of your own or follow a section, or the whole route, of one of the long distance cycle ways that pass through the area (see diagram p.7).

Remember that the Dales weather can be inhospitable, even in the summer months, so ensure you have packed wind and waterproof clothing. Other items to take include a bicycle pump and a basic repair kit, with multi-headed spanner and patches for punctures. (A spare inner tube saves road side repairs). It is more comfortable and safer to carry luggage in panniers or saddlebags than in a rucksack.

There are long stretches without shops so always carry plenty of food and drink. Lights and reflectors are a must even if you plan to reach your destination before nightfall. Bright or reflective clothing makes good sense because visibility may sometimes be poor.

Before starting out, make sure your cycle is in a well-maintained condition. Pay particular attention to the brakes. Some routes are extremely steep (1 in 4 or 25%) and great care is needed when going downhill, particularly with a laden cycle in wet weather. On some hills it is necessary to take extreme caution. Although much of the cycling available in the area is along minor roads, traffic can be heavy at times in the summer. Take care especially when cycling on main roads.

The HARVEY map Yorkshire Dales for Cyclists at 1:100,000 scale is designed especially with the touring cyclist in mind (see p.5).

MOUNTAIN BIKING

The Dales also provide a massive variety of challenging mountain bike routes from moorland traverses, old mining tracks, green lanes and single-tracks, which can all be combined to give routes of different lengths and difficulties.

Specific maps and guides are available from National Park Centres. HARVEY Outdoor Maps highlight off road cycle routes in accordance with the CTC's off road grades to enable cyclists to plan their day (see p.5).

RAIL AND BUS TRAVEL WITH CYCLES

It is possible to take cycles on the train to Ikley and Skipton. For other services contact National Rail enquiries tel: 08457 484950.

A few buses carry bikes. Check with National Traveline tel: 0870 608 2608 or www.dalesbus.org for times.

CYCLE PARKING

Cycle stands for securing your bike are available at National Park Centres, in town centres and at many attractions. This network is being expanded. There are also cycle lockers available at Grassington National Park Centre and Ilkley station.

CYCLE SHOPS

Arthur Caygill Cycles, Richmond	tel: 01748 825469
Ace Cycles, Harrogate	tel: 01423 508417
Boneshakers, Harrogate	tel: 01423 709453
Cawthorn Cycle, Harrogate	tel: 01423 888846
Chevin Cycles, Otley	tel: 01943 462773
Cycle Way, Harrogate	tel: 01423 566215
J.D. Cycles, Ilkley	tel: 01943 816101
Moonglu, Ripon	tel: 01765 601106
Nidderdale Motors, Pateley Bridge	tel: 01423 711309
Psychlosport, Harrogate	tel: 01423 545413
Kirkby Stephen Cycle Centre, Kirkby Stephen	tel: 01768 371658
Dave Ferguson Cycles, Skipton	tel: 01756 795367
Settle Cycles, Station Yard, Settle	tel: 01729 822216
Skipton Bicycle Shop, Skipton	tel: 01756 794386

CYCLE HIRE

Dales Mountain Bike Hire, Fremington	tel: 01748 884356
Wensleydale Bike Hire, Castle Bolton	tel: 01969 623981
Kirkby Stephen Cycle Centre, Kirkby Stephen	tel: 01768 371658
Dave Ferguson Cycles, Skipton	tel: 01756 795367
Kettlewell Garage, Kettlewell	tel: 01756 760225 (& spares)
Skipton Bicycle Shop, Skipton	tel: 01756 794386

LONG DISTANCE CYCLE ROUTES IN THE YORKSHIRE DALES

Yorkshire Dales Cycle Way (NY10) is a challenging 210km (130 mile) circular route visiting most of the major dales. It is designed to start and finish in Skipton. However the route can be started at any point, or divided into sections to suit the individual cyclist. Many will find it is ideal for a leisurely six day tour. A link to Ilkley (unsigned) has also been included for those wishing to start or finish there. A specific map of the route is available from HARVEY (see p.5).

The following cycle routes partly run through the Yorkshire Dales:

Pennine Cycleway (NCN68) is a 580km (350 mile) route running from Derby on the southern edge of the Peak District to Berwick on Tweed on the Scottish border. Details are available at www.sustrans.org.uk.

Cumbria Cycleway (CCW) is a 418km (261 mile) route around the edge of Cumbria. Details are available from relevant tourist information centres.

West Yorkshire Cycle Route (WYCR) is a 240km (150 mile) circular route that roughly follows the West Yorkshire County Boundary. A laminated map is available free from Leeds City Council, Dept. of Highways & Transportation, Leonardo Building, 2 Rossington Street, Leeds LS2 8HB. (send A5 SAE).

National Byway Cycle Route (NBCR) is a 6400km (4000 mile) leisure cycle route around Britain which passes through the eastern edge of the Yorkshire Dales. Details from www.thenationalbyway.org

Northallerton - Penrith (NCN71) is nearly finalised and is due to be launched in 2004. The route as it stands in 2003 is marked in this atlas.

Colours and Symbols on the Maps

There is a full key on p.113. The following pages give further explanation of how the symbols are used on HARVEY mapping. Items in purple are as written in the key. The sample opposite shows the use of many of the symbols.

Roads, tracks and paths are differentiated for easy recognition. A road is always tarmac. A track might be a current vehicle track, an old railway line (currently with visible path) or a forest road. A disused railway with no visible path is shown with a grey symbol. A footpath is sufficiently clear to be found/followed even in poor weather conditions. An intermittent path is a small path followable in good conditions but might be difficult to follow at times and might be crossed unnoticed. In any area there will always be a multitude of small paths and animal trails which are not shown on the map.

No attempt is normally made to distinguish between public and private roads, although as a general rule, roads with coloured infill are public. However, rights of way (public footpaths, bridleways and byways) are shown. The appropriate right of way symbol is used together with/without a footpath or track symbol, depending on whether the path is visible on the ground or not. Permissive paths are shown.

The black symbol for a boundary may indicate a wall or fence. Where the boundary is in a ruinous state and therefore not as easy to find/follow, the symbol becomes grey. As far as possible all boundaries on moorland and rough pasture are shown. However new fences may be erected and their inclusion will have to await the next revision of the map. No attempt is made to distinguish between high deer fences and others. Within improved pasture (the darker yellow on the map) boundaries are not shown.

Watercourses, shown in blue, are categorised according to how easy they are to cross. A narrow stream can be stepped over. A wide stream will not be crossable with dry feet without searching for a suitable point. A river would certainly involve getting wet unless you find a bridge. The wider the river, the broader the symbol. Footbridges are generally shown over rivers or wide streams. Bear in mind that they may disappear after severe flooding.

Ground which is basically wet for all but the driest of seasons is shown as marsh. Ground which is peaty and wet with deeply eroded channels is a severe hindrance and large areas are shown with the special symbol peat hag.

The height, shape and slope of the ground is shown in great detail with contours at a 15m interval. Every fifth (index) contour is heavier to make height calculation easier. Auxiliary contour lines (form lines) are added to show features missed by the standard contours. They are approximately half way in height between the contour lines. Layer colouring is added to help identify the higher ground.

Where the ground is covered by vegetation the contours are brown. Where the ground becomes predominantly rocky outcrops and small crags the contours change to grey. The use of grey contours avoids the shape of the ground being masked by a multitude of crag symbols. An area shown with grey contours indicates that caution is required. It may be possible to find a route when ascending, but could be dangerous when descending, especially in bad weather.

Major crags are shown with a separate symbol. They definitely indicate no-go areas for walkers. Significant large boulders are marked individually as they can be used for navigation. Boulder field, stony ground and scree are shown where such areas pose significant obstacles to progress.

Only large significant cairns are shown. They are generally only found on summits and prominent geographical features.

Yellow is used to highlight farmland and other cultivated land. Two categories are used, improved pasture and rough pasture. For the walker, access through farmland is always sensitive. The indication of the extent of farmland and routes/rights of way is intended to help the walker. If in doubt about access the farmer/landowner should always be approached.

Woodland/forest can be a major obstacle to the hillwalker. To give access through forest HARVEY maps clearly distinguish between forest roads, rides and footpaths. Rides are linear breaks through the trees. Firebreaks can be regarded as wide rides. Rides give access through the forest but may be very wet and heavy going. The forest is also graded into categories. Using two shades of green, the map distinguishes between dense plantation (predominantly conifer) and open forest (predominantly broadleaf) woodland.

There is also information on the location of car parks, campsites, youth hostels, public telephones, public toilets, places of interest, nature reserves, etc.

In principle, the features on the map are the ones visible on the ground. However, the boundary of the National Park and of the Area of Outstanding Natural Beauty are included. Long distance cycle routes and long distance paths/National Trails are indicated.

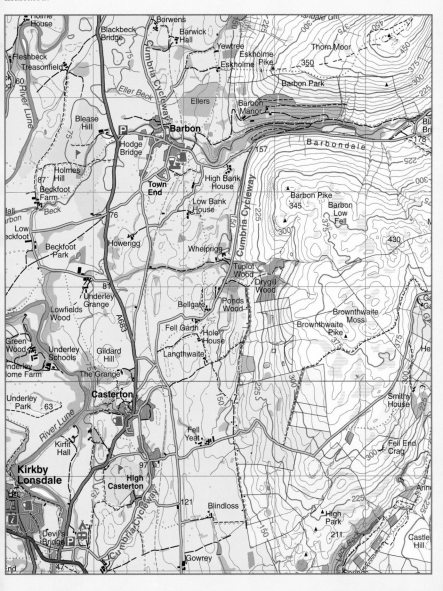

For local tourist information contact:

Grassington	tel: 01756 752774
Horton in Ribblesdale	tel: 01729 860333
Ingleton	tel: 01524 241049
Kirkby Lonsdale	tel: 01524 271437
Kirkby Stephen	tel: 01768 371199
Malham	tel: 01729 830363
Sedbergh	tel: 01539 620125
Settle	tel: 01729 825192
Skipton	tel: 01756 792809

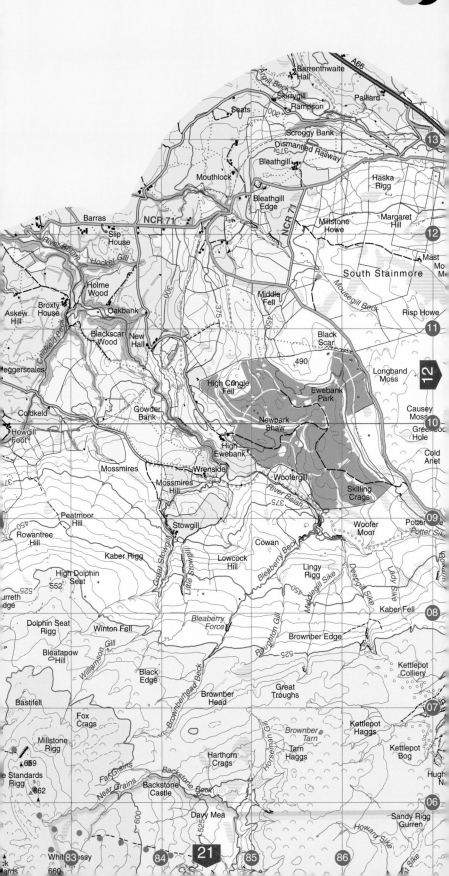

Bow

Castle

A67

Gilmon

West Gates

Whor

Swinholme

Pennine Way

Lady Myres

West Charity Farm

High Green Fell

East Mellwaters

A66

Dismantled Railway

320

West Mellwaters

The Trough

Hug Gill

Huggill Sike

365

375

Gilmonby Moor

Chert Gill

375

12

11

13

10

Trough Heads

Wytham Moor

Seven Hills

Seven Hills Tarn

402

Sweet Sike

375

Suet Set Hills

Hazel Bush Hill

Elfer Beck Rigg

Bog Scar

Bar Gap

446

Citron Seat

375

Hunt Rove Gill

Sleightholme

Skitter Hill

Charl Gill

Redmire Hills

Black Hill

Scargill High Moor

East Black

West Black Sike

Pike Hill

Bow Hills

09

Coney Seat Hill

Crook Siker Gill

Ling Pulled Hill

Bleakhow Edge

Tarnhow Hill

White Crag Moss

White Crag

Great Foster Hill

Faggergill Moss

Rushy Moor

Mudbeck Hill

Limestone Hill

Long Rigg

Little Foster Hill

Seavy Hill

National Park

08

West Moor

Adjustment Sike

Mud Beck

Green Hill

Dale Head Common

Cleasby Hill

A50

Seavy Hill

Faggergill Moor

The Howl

Black S

375

Leading Stead Bottom

430

Ravens Park

Greystone Edge

07

idge

208

Dale Head

Hill Top Farm

High Faggergill

Smithson H

Leadingstead

06

Arkengarthdale Moor

375

Park Head

Gale Head Moor

Piper Knot

Roe Beck

96

97

24

98

99

Shepherd's Lodg

Kitle Hill

Seal House Moor

Low F

For local tourist information contact:

Harrogate	tel: 01423 537300
Ingleton	tel: 01524 241049
Kirkby Lonsdale	tel: 01524 271437
Kirkby Stephen	tel: 01768 371199
Richmond	tel: 01748 850252
Ripon	tel: 01765 604625
Sedbergh	tel: 01539 620125
Settle	tel: 01729 825192
Skipton	tel: 01756 792809

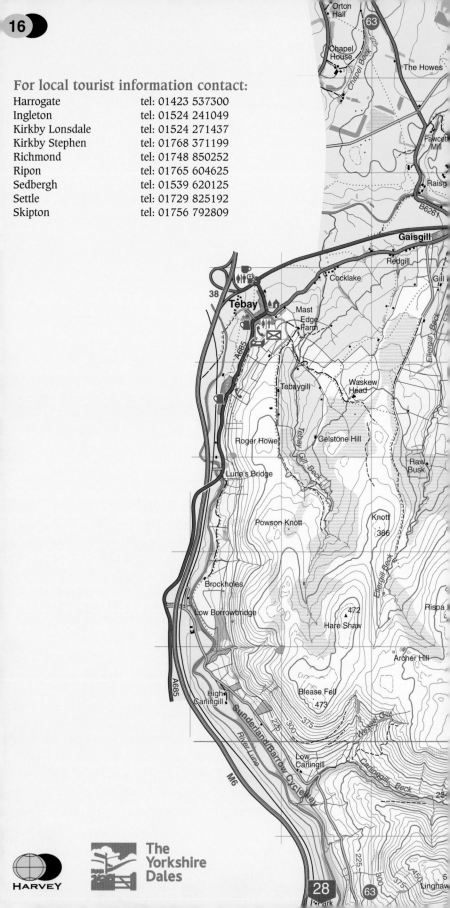

HARVEY

The Yorkshire Dales

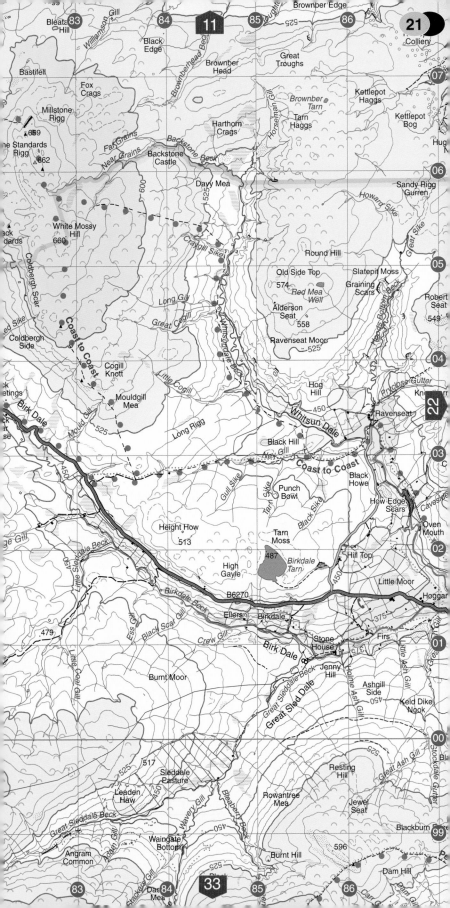

28

SEDBERGH

National Park Centre
Castlehaw Tower
Marthwaite
A684
A683
Borrett
Birks

500m

16

62   63

97

Brow Head
Top Wood
Grayrigg Head
Simgill
Cowperthwaite
Coat-o'-West
Beanthwaite End

96

Wythmoor
Holme Park Farm
Lakethwaite
Birchfield

Sunderland/Barrow Cycleway

95

Lambrigg Park Farm
Green Dykes

94

Lambrigg Park

Moorcock Hall

Firbank Fell

Ellershaw Moss

Owshaw Hill

93

37

Drybeck Hill

Dales Way

High House
Lowgill Viaduct
Crook of Lune Bridge
Davy Bank
124
Crook of Lune

Railway Terrace

Midgehole
Fairmile Gate

Mire Head

Brunt Sike

Beck Hous

Ridding

Four Lane Ends

Beck Foot

Moors
Bowers
Oakbank
Thwaite
Birkhaw

Hole House
Goodies
Syke

Hill Top
324

Fox's Pulpit
307 Knotts
Underknotts

Branthwaite

River Lune

Party Haw
Heatherlea
Whinny Haw
Lune Viaduct
Ford

New Field
Waller Heights
Ghyll Farm
Lincolns Inn Bridge
Garths

B6257

A684
Capplethwaite Hall
White Hall
Luneside
Ingmire Hall

Dales Way

Hebblethwaites

High Oaks
Killington New Bridge
Holme

Grassrigg

The Hill

Greenholme

62   40   63

Low Park

Fairmile Beck

Whins E

Lingl

225   300   375   450

Pennine Cycleway

Cumbria Way

HARVEY

Maps of other popular walking
areas available. For up to date
information, visit our Web shop:
www.harveymaps.co.uk
or call our hotline: 01786 841202

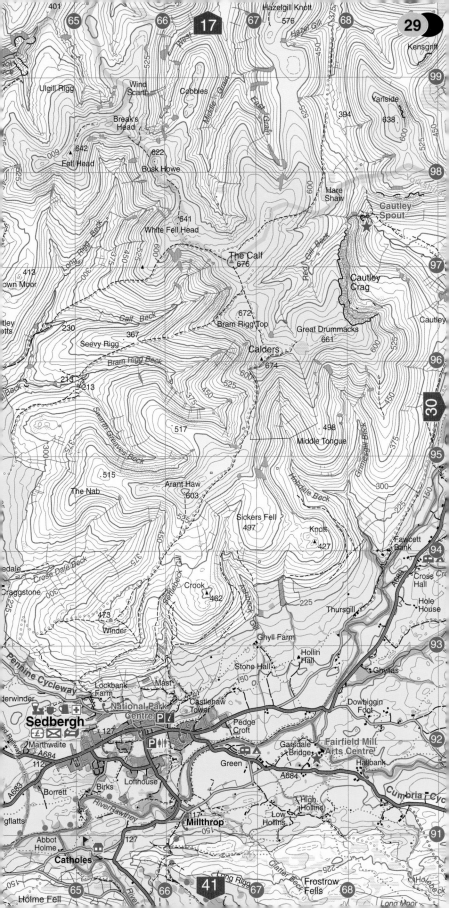

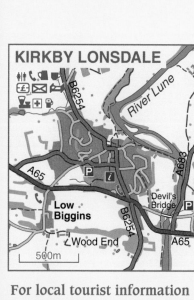

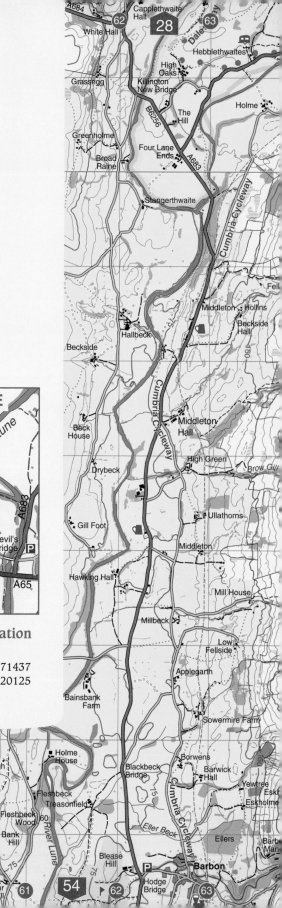

For local tourist information contact:

Kirkby Lonsdale   tel: 01524 271437
Sedbergh   tel: 01539 620125

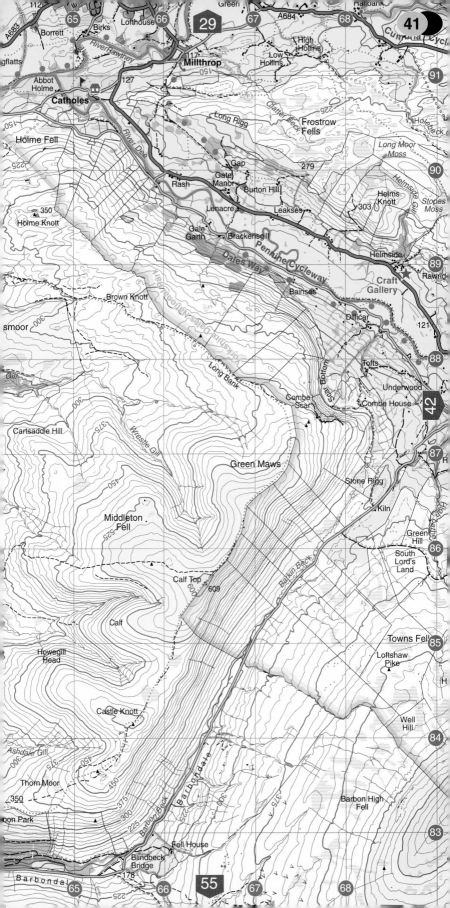

Black Quarry

Moor Quarry

Shawl Wood

Leyburn

A684

150

150

Candle Workshop

Teddy Bear Shop

Harmby

Tea Pottery

Cracken House

ensley idge

17

Howe Hills

A6108

River Ure

Gale Bank

150

Oak Wood

The Parks

150

Middleham

88

52

Park Farm

Sharp Hill Farm

Castle

133

236

Cross Bank

Naylor's Hill

Middleham Low Moor

225

William's Hill Ring & Bailey

87

35

Cotescue Park

Ever Bank

Manor House Farm

hgill

Thorngill

ongill

upgill

The bidden orner 172

Coverham Abbey

Holme Hill

Hullo Bridge

150

Cover Scar

Yorkshire Dales National

East Witton Lodge

Bird Ridding Farm

Cherry Hill

Barn

Hanghow Pastures

225

Braithwaite Hall

Cockhill Low Wood

150

Witton Banks

86

Ashes

Castle Steads

300

Braithwaite Banks

Caldbergh

235

351

Crundell Hill

413

375

Braithwaite Moor

350

Witton Fell

85

Caldbergh Gill

Grey Stone Flat

Tom Claypham Beck

84

man ure

Red Way

422

Jenny Binks Moss

Brown Rigg

375

Ulfers

Caldbergh Moor

idiman row

389

Long Side

Lobley Crags

Agra Moor 329

Backsstone Gill

Bardley Beck

Brown Beck Crags

83

10

Ulfers Gill

11

65

12

13

Dales Cycle W...

LEYBURN

500m

Beech End
Interactive
Model Village

Teddy Bear
Shop

Tea Pottery

Harmby
Cracken
House

For local tourist information contact:

Leyburn	tel: 01969 623069
Aysgarth	tel: 01969 663424
Hawes	tel: 01969 667450

Middleham

88

51

87

Cover Bridge

River Ure

Fleets
House

Yorkshire Dales National Park

East
Witton

East Witton
Mill

86

150

Low Thorpe

Jervaulx
Abbey

Witton Banks

Waterloo
Farm

143

Lea Gill Beck

NBCR

Thirsting
Castle
Lodge

Low
Newstead

High Jervaulx

85

350

Witton Fell

Hammer
Farm

NBCR

High Newstead

150

Deep Gill Beck

84

Tom Claypham Beck

Sowden
Beck

Horse
Riding

243

Ellings

Witton Moor

Tranmire
Hill

Ellingstring
Plantation

83

gra Moor 329

Tranmire

300

267 Swinney Beck

Brown Beck
Crags

NBCR

300

14

15

66

16

Bales

17

Long Distance Cycle Routes passing through the Yorkshire Dales

The Yorkshire Dales Cycle Way (NY10)

This is a challenging 210km (130 mile) circular route visiting most of the major dales. It is designed to start and finish in Skipton. However the route can be started at any point, or divided into sections to suit every cyclist. Many will find it is ideal for a leisurely six day tour. A link to Ilkley (unsigned) has also been included for those wishing to start or finish there. A specific map of the route is available from HARVEY: www.harveymaps.co.uk.

The Pennine Cycleway (NCN68) is a 580km (350 mile) route running from Derby on the southern edge of the Peak District to Berwick on Tweed on the Scottish border. Details are available at www.sustrans.org.uk.

The Cumbria Cycleway (CCW) is a 418km (261 mile) route around the edge of Cumbria. Details are available from relevant tourist information centres.

The West Yorkshire Cycle Route (WYCR) is a 240km (150 mile) circular route that roughly follows the West Yorkshire County Boundary. A laminated map is available free from Leeds City Council, Dept. of Highways & Transportation, Leonardo Building, 2 Rossington Street, Leeds LS2 8HB. (send A5 SAE).

The National Byway Cycle Route (NBCR) is a 6400km (4000 mile) leisure cycle route around Britain which passes through the eastern edge of the Yorkshire Dales. Details from www.thenationalbyway.org

Northallerton - Penrith (NCN71) is nearly finalised and is due to be launched in 2004. The route as it stands in 2003 is marked on the map.

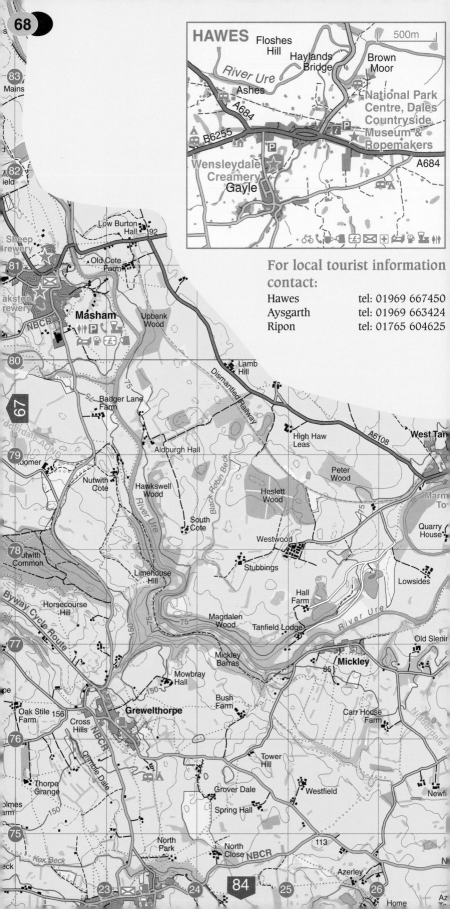

HAWES

Floshes Hill
Haylands Bridge
Brown Moor
River Ure
Ashes
A684
National Park Centre, Dales Countryside Museum & Ropemakers
B6255
A684
Wensleydale Creamery
Gayle

500m

For local tourist information contact:

Hawes   tel: 01969 667450
Aysgarth   tel: 01969 663424
Ripon   tel: 01765 604625

83
Mains
82
ield
Sheep rewery
81
akston rewery
NBCR
Masham
Upbank Wood
80
67
dderdale AONB
79
oomer
Nutwith Cote
Hawkswell Wood
South Cote
River Ure
78
utwith Common
Limehouse Hill
Horsecourse Hill
Byway Cycle Route
77
Mowbray Hall
Oak Stile Farm
156
Cross Hills
NBCR
76
Crimble Dale
pe
Thorpe Grange
olmes arm
150
75
ck
Kex Beck
23
24

Low Burton Hall
192
Old Cote Farm
Lamb Hill
Dismantled Railway
75
Badger Lane Farm
Aldburgh Hall
High Haw Leas
A6108
West Tan
75
Peter Wood
Heslett Wood
Marm To
Quarry House
Westwood
Stubbings
Lowsides
Hall Farm
River Ure
Magdalen Wood
Tanfield Lodge
75
150
Old Slenir
Mickley Barras
85
Mickley
Bush Farm
Carr House Farm
Grewelthorpe
150
Tower Hill
Grover Dale
Westfield
Newfi
Spring Hall
North Park
North Close
NBCR
113
Azerley
Home
84
25
26

500m

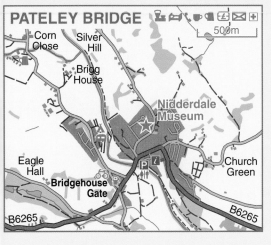

PATELEY BRIDGE

500m

Corn Close
Silver Hill
Brigg House
Nidderdale Museum
Eagle Hall
Bridgehouse Gate
Church Green
B6265
B6265

For local tourist
information contact:

Pateley Bridge	tel: 01423 711147
Richmond	tel: 01748 850252
Bedale:	tel: 01677 424604
Leyburn	tel: 01969 623069
Reeth	tel: 01748 884059
Ripon	tel: 01765 604625

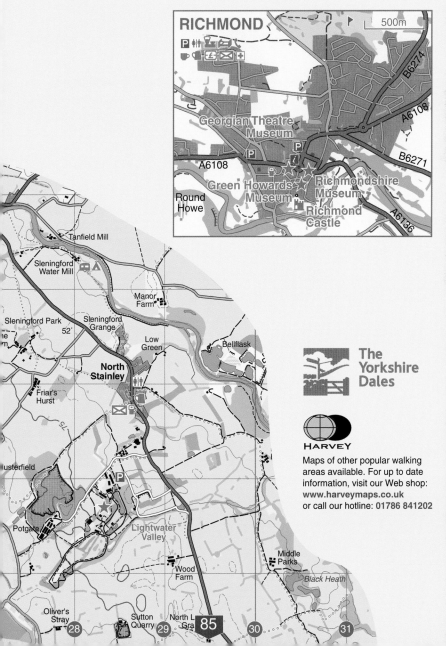

RICHMOND

500m

B6274
A6108
B6271
B6136

Georgian Theatre Museum
A6108
Green Howards Museum
Round Howe
Richmondshire Museum
Richmond Castle

Tanfield Mill
Sleningford Water Mill
Manor Farm
Sleningford Park
Sleningford Grange
52'
Low Green
Bellflask
North Stainley
Friar's Hurst
usterfield
Potgate
Lightwater Valley
Wood Farm
Middle Parks
Black Heath
Oliver's Stray
Sutton Quarry
North L Gra

28   29   **85**   30   31

The Yorkshire Dales

HARVEY

Maps of other popular walking
areas available. For up to date
information, visit our Web shop:
www.harveymaps.co.uk
or call our hotline: **01786 841202**

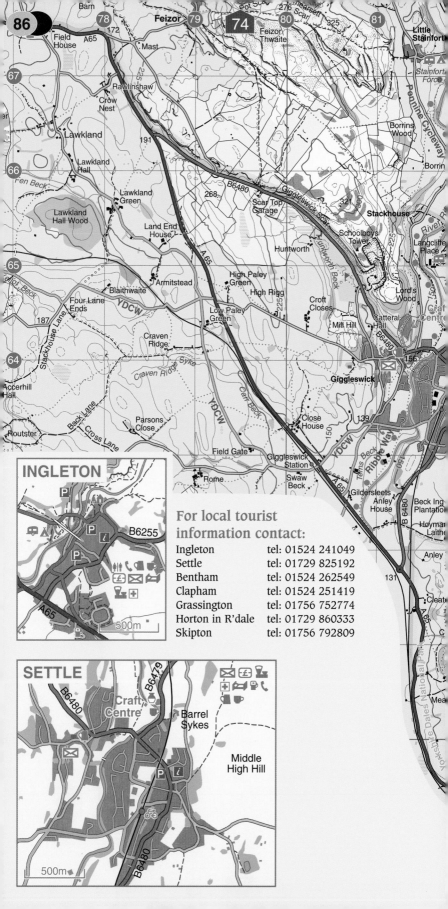

Barn
Feizor 78 79 74 80 81
172 Feizor Thwaite Little Stainforth
A65 Field House Mast Stainforth Force
67 Rawlinshaw Pennine Cycleway
Crow Nest Borrins Wood
Lawkland 191 Borrin
Lawkland Hall Borrin
66 Lawkland Green B6480 Giggleswick Scar Stackhouse
Fen Beck 268 Scar Top Garage 321 Schoolboys Tower River
Lawkland Hall Wood Land End House Huntworth Langcliffe Place
65 Armitstead High Paley Green Lord's Wood Craf Centr
Blaithwaite High Rigg Croft Closes Catteral Hall
Four Lane Ends YDCW Low Paley Green Mill Hill B6480
187 Craven Ridge Giggleswick 156
64 Stackhouse Lane Craven Ridge Syke Carr Beck YDCW
Accerhill Hall Parsons Close YDCW Close House 139
Routster Back Lane Cross Lane Field Gate Giggleswick Station 150 Ribble Way
Rome Swaw Beck Gildersleets Anley House Beck Ing Plantation
Hoyma Laithe
Anley
131
Cleat

INGLETON

P B6255

500m

A65

For local tourist information contact:

Ingleton	tel: 01524 241049
Settle	tel: 01729 825192
Bentham	tel: 01524 262549
Clapham	tel: 01524 251419
Grassington	tel: 01756 752774
Horton in R'dale	tel: 01729 860333
Skipton	tel: 01756 792809

SETTLE

B6479
B6480
Craft Centre
Barrel Sykes
Middle High Hill
P
500m
B6480

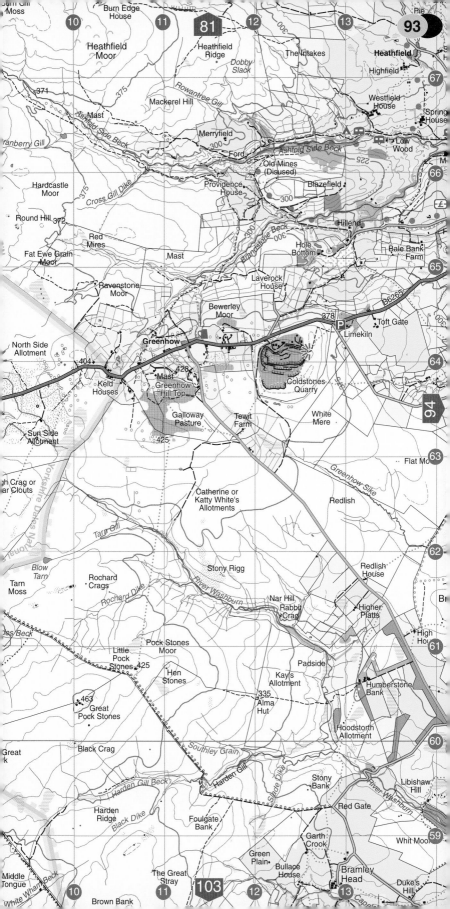

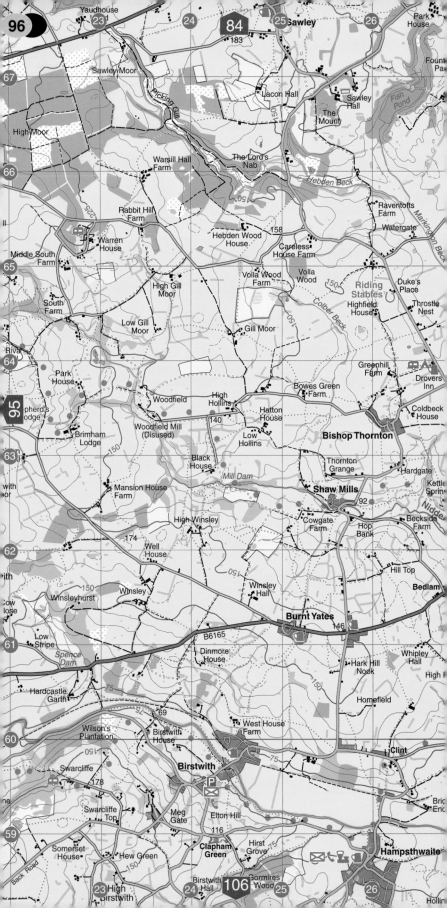

GRASSINGTON

Museum

National Park Centre

Linton Falls

B6265

500m

For local tourist information contact:

Grassington	tel: 01756 752774
Bentham	tel: 01524 262549
Clapham	tel: 01524 251419
Horton in Ribblesdale	tel: 01729 860333
Ingleton	tel: 01524 241049
Settle	tel: 01729 825192
Skipton	tel: 01756 792809

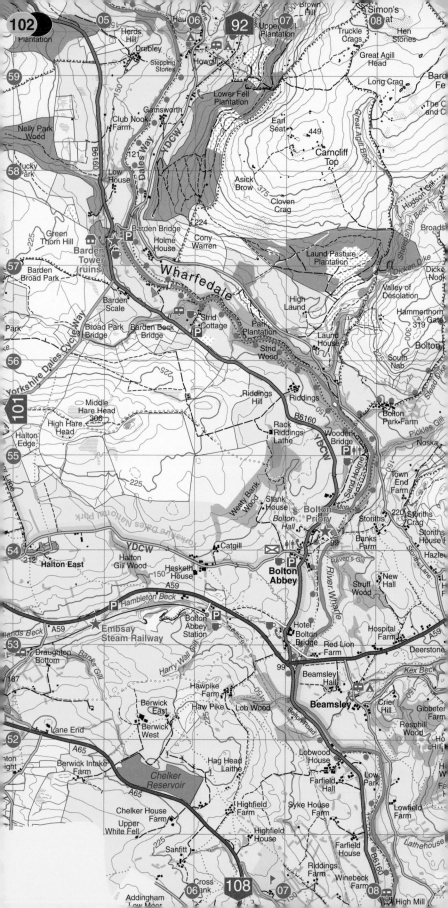

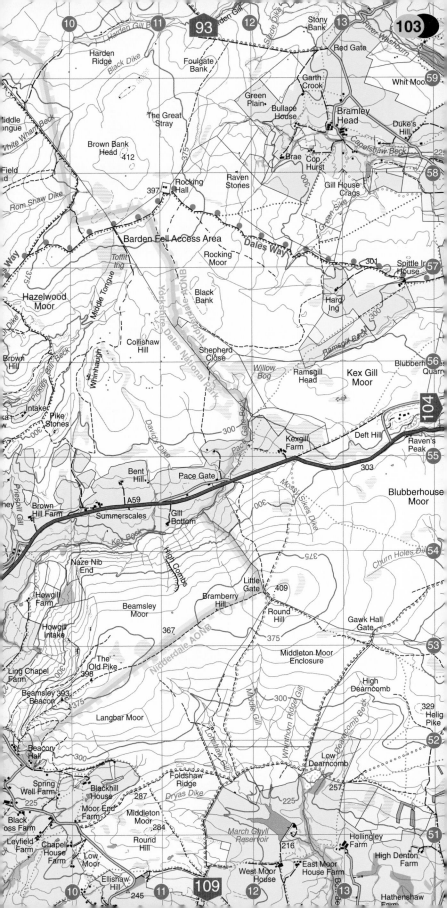

For local tourist information contact:

Skipton	tel: 01756 792809
Bentham	tel: 01524 262549
Clapham	tel: 01524 251419
Harrogate	tel: 01423 537300
Horton in R'dale	tel: 01729 860333
Ingleton	tel: 01524 241049
Ilkley	tel: 01943 602319
Malham	tel: 01729 830363
Otley	tel: 0113 2477707
Settle	tel: 01729 825192

NATIONAL GRID
The grid in this atlas is the National Grid. A grid reference (GR) is a way of pin-pointing a unique square on any map using the National Grid. A grid reference consists of distance east (Easting) followed by distance north (Northing).

2 letters found on the overview map (p.1)
  easting on N or S edge of each map
    tenths eastward
SD 108510 GR of Round Hill (p109)
      tenths northward
    northing on W or E edge
    of each map

This GR with 2 letters and 6 numbers (6 fig GR) pinpoints a 100m square.

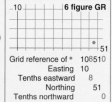

	6 figure GR
Grid reference of	108510
Easting	10
Tenths eastward	8
Northing	51
Tenths northward	0

GPS (Global Positioning System)

This atlas can be used with GPS. Set your GPS receiver to Map Datum OSGB and the Position Format to British Grid. To obtain a 10 metre GR, further tenths must be estimated and added after both easting and northing to give an 8 figure GR. (Round Hill SD 1088 5106)

Note
1 GPS accuracy can be variable.
2 Where several features are close together, symbols may be displaced for clarity. Positional map accuracy greater than 10m is not guaranteed.

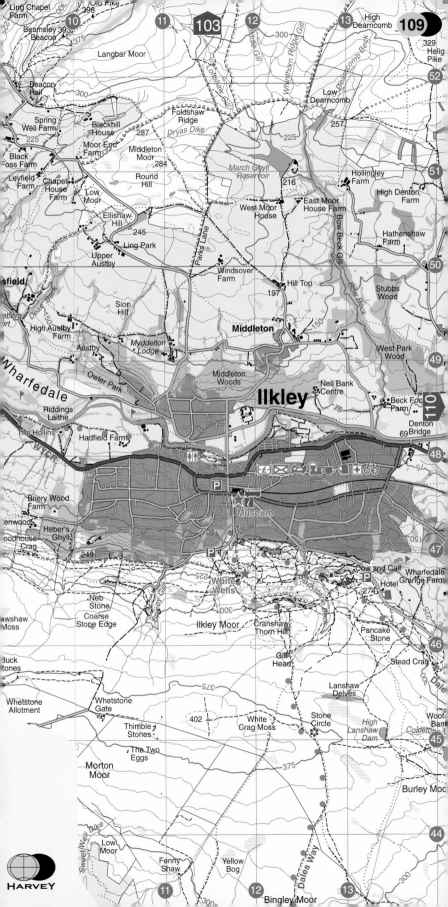

Index to place names

This gazetteer contains settlements and major geographical features within the Dales.
The first double number for each entry is the page number; the group of four numbers identifies the grid square in which the centre point of the feature falls.